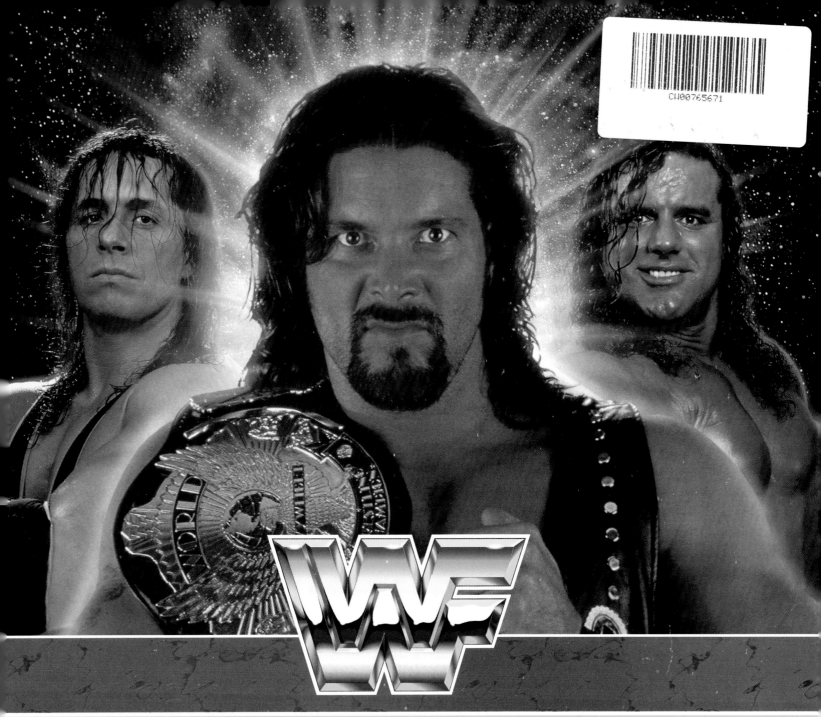

WWF

WRESTLING

A LIVE-ACTION LOOK AT THE SUPERSTARS OF THE WORLD WRESTLING FEDERATION

EDITED BY **VINCE RUSSO** OF THE WORLD WRESTLING FEDERATION MAGAZINE

Virgin

PRODUCED BY CARLTON BOOKS

First published in 1995 by
Virgin Publishing Limited
332 Ladbroke Grove
London W10 5AH

Printed and bound in Spain

A catalogue record for this book is available from the British Library

ISBN 0.86369.971.5

Edited by: Vince Russo, World Wrestling Magazine
Writing contributions: Keith Elliot Greenberg
Project editor: Tim Smith
Design: Rob Fairclough, Susie Hooper
Production: Garry Lewis

Portions of this book were written by World Wrestling Federation Magazine

Special thanks to Bob Mitchell, Tricia Breheney, Midge Bacon,
TitanSports Publications.

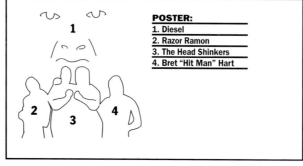

POSTER:
1. Diesel
2. Razor Ramon
3. The Head Shinkers
4. Bret "Hit Man" Hart

CONTENTS

The Royal Rumble shakes the Earth
each winter. In 1995, the Royal Rumble will go down
at the Sun Dome in Tampa.

The King of the Ring pay-per-view spectacular
made its debut in 1993 from Dayton, Ohio.

SummerSlam, the annual rite of summer, has been on
the Federation's pay-per-view calendar since 1988.

WrestleMania is the grand-daddy of all pay-per-view events.
WrestleMania XI is coming up in April 1995.

INTRODUCTION

Spectacle, emotion, roller-coaster excitement, larger than life, world champion athletes; these are all essential aspects of the greatest sports organization anywhere in the world: the World Wrestling Federation.

From the awesome Survivor Series, the world-famous Wrestle Mania and the adrenaline-pumping SummerSlam to the regal King of the Ring and the staggering Royal Rumble, the World Wrestling Federation extravaganza thrills everybody who has eyes to see, ears to hear and lungs to yell with, all over the world.

This book looks into the histories and ambitions of some of the finest superstars ever to grace the world-famous squared circle. We all know that it's amazing to watch these fabulous athletes excel in their craft, but it's even better getting the inside track on what makes Diesel, British Bulldog, the Hit Man, the Undertaker, and the other 20 wrestlers featured in this essential guide work their magic.

You'll feel as if you're in the ring with your favorite World Wrestling Federation superstars when you dip into these pages...

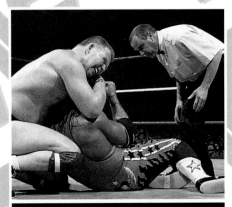

The Survivor Series is a team-oriented event in which teams of superstars strive to survive.

"It's Big Daddy Cool time!"

Diesel is a man known far and wide as Big Daddy Cool. He's also known as the Federation Champion.

DIESEL

ALL REVVED UP WITH SOMEPLACE TO GO!

It may have been the biggest upset in World Wrestling Federation history. On November 26, 1994, big Diesel stood in the ring at New York's Madison Square Garden, staring down on World Wrestling Federation Champion Bob Backlund. Three days earlier at the Survivor Series, Backlund had recaptured the belt he'd held from 1978 to 1984. He vowed that his second reign would be just as long.

However, Diesel had other plans. As the bell rang, the nearly 7-foot-tall gladiator caught Backlund in the midsection with a kick. Before Backlund had a chance to react, the 317-pound challenger wrapped his arms around the champ, flipping him upside down and crashing him into the mat with his infamous Jackknife.

The referee dropped to the canvas and counted—Diesel had won the World Wrestling Federation Championship in a record eight seconds!

In his short time in the World Wrestling Federation, Diesel has gone where few have ventured. Big Daddy Cool, as he's sometimes called, started out as a bodyguard for Shawn Michaels, but fans quickly decided that he was destined for better things. Soon, people were paying more attention to Diesel than Michaels, and the duo had a falling out—with the fans firmly in Diesel's corner.

The championship victory made Diesel one of an elite group. He, Bret "Hit Man" Hart and Pedro Morales are the only Federation superstars in history ever to hold the triple crown—by capturing the World Wrestling Federation Title, the Intercontinental Title and Tag Team Title. Where does he go from here? With his youth, strength and motivation, the future is limitless.

RIGHT: BIG DADDY COOL DIESEL captured the World Wrestling Federation Title from Bob Backlund in late November 1994.

DIESEL

NICKNAME:	Big Daddy Cool
HOME TOWN:	Las Vegas, Nevada
HEIGHT:	Near 7'
WEIGHT:	317 pounds
MOTTO:	It's Big Daddy Cool time!

Bob Backlund is a former two-time World Wrestling Federation Champion.

BOB BACKLUND

EMPEROR OF THE OLD GENERATION

Bob Backlund personifies what he proudly calls the Old Generation of World Wrestling Federation performers. At 45 years old, he longs for what he calls "the golden days" of professional wrestling.

A onetime college standout, the 6-foot-2-inch, 234-pound Backlund snared the World Wrestling Federation Title in 1978. For seven years, he defended the belt all over the world, selling out arenas everywhere.

At the 1994 Survivor Series, Mr. Backlund (as he likes to be called) received a form of poetic justice when he recaptured the championship from the symbol of the New Generation, Bret "Hit Man" Hart, but Backlund's victory was bittersweet. Just two days later at New York's Madison Square Garden, the mighty Diesel Jackknifed the title away from the newly crowned champ in the record time of eight seconds.

Predictably enough, Backlund now screams "conspiracy" and vows to punish the rest of the World Wrestling Federation for the loss by placing everyone he wrestles in his patented cross-face chicken-wing!

RIGHT: Mr. Bob Backlund despises everything in the New Generation, especially Diesel and Bret Hart.

BOB BACKLUND	
NICKNAME:	Champ
HOME TOWN:	Princeton, Minnesota
HEIGHT:	6'2"
WEIGHT:	234 pounds
MOTTO:	I'm not a plebeian!

KING KONG BUNDY

THE WALKING CONDOMINIUM

King Kong Bundy polishes off his opponents with the mighty Avalanche.

The bald-headed son of Atlantic City, New Jersey, grew up in the shadow of the beach town's famed casinos. Under the boardwalk, he watched henchmen for the bookmakers shake down losing customers.

In the World Wrestling Federation, he could have simply relied on his incredible dimensions—he's 6-foot-1 and 444 pounds—to gain triumph after triumph. However, like the folks who'd mortgaged their homes for the chance to score big in Atlantic City, Bundy wouldn't accept a win unless it was spectacular. He told all referees that he wasn't satisfied to cover an opponent for the count of three. Instead, he wanted a five-count.

Bundy was one of the most terrifying men in the World Wrestling Federation in the mid-1980s. Then he mysteriously vanished. In 1994, he returned, more brutal than ever.

With Million Dollar Man Ted DiBiase now managing him, it's likely that the chrome-domed behemoth will continue gambling between the ropes and taking home everything in the pot.

RIGHT: King Kong Bundy is a walking mastodon who tips the scales at 444 pounds.

Bret "Hit Man" Hart has done it all in the World Wrestling Federation.

BRET HART

NICKNAME: Hit Man
HOME TOWN: Calgary, Canada
HEIGHT: 6'
WEIGHT: 234 pounds
MOTTO: I'm the best there is, the best there was and the best there ever will be.

BRET "HIT MAN" HART

THE EXCELLENCE OF EXECUTION

No man in the history of the World Wrestling Federation has ever achieved the standards reached by Bret "Hit Man" Hart. Many wrestling authorities go as far as to say that no man ever will! Bret Hart is one of only three men to have captured the triple crown of wrestling (Federation Champion, Intercontinental Champion and Tag Team Champion). While that feat in itself is amazing, what makes it legendary is that the Hit Man captured each title not once, but TWICE! Throughout his career, Bret has had the reputation of being a man who backs down from no one. Backed by a devastating finishing move that he calls the Sharpshooter, Bret has graciously accepted the challenge of every one of his opponents. With his unique blend of heart, determination, ring prowess and power, this ring technician looks as if he'll be dominating the squared circle for a long time to come!

LEFT: The Hit Man Bret Hart is a two-time World Wrestling Federation Champion.

●●●●●●●●●●●●●●●●●●●●

THE BRET HART TRIVIA QUIZ

Test your knowledge of the World Wrestling Federation's most consistent athlete with this special brain-slamming Bret Hart quiz!

1 Bret's dad, Stu, was a champion athlete. He wrestled and played what sport professionally?

2 Bret's mom, Helen, was the daughter of what flamboyant U.S. Olympian?

3 How did Helen and Stu spend their honeymoon?

4 Where does the Hart clan still reside?

5 What is Stu's Dungeon?

6 Bret won his first title while he was a member of the Hart Foundation. Whom did the Harts defeat to capture the Tag Team Championship?

7 They had a little help from the referee, though. He subsequently joined them for a spell. Do you remember who that was?

8 Whom did they beat for their second title?

9 The team's favorite finisher was dubbed the Hart Attack. How did it involve Bret?

10 Bret decided to go his own way after the Harts lost to the Nasty Boys at what WrestleMania?

11 Bret had immediate success as a singles competitor, as he quickly grabbed the Intercontinental Title. Whom did he defeat (a man with few flaws) for this title?

12 Hart's second Intercontinental Title came at the expense of a longtime family friend — he would later lend Bret a hand at WrestleMania X. Can you tell us who that was?

13 Next for Bret was a date with Ric Flair for the World Wrestling Federation Championship. Flair wasn't about to hand it to him, though. How did Hart finally finish him off?

14 By beating Flair, the Hit Man became the first Canadian to take the Federation's top prize. Is that true or false?

15 The Hit Man also earned another distinction. What was that?

16 Bret didn't rest on his laurels. He defended the Federation Championship at the 1992 Survivor Series, where he took on the reigning Intercontinental Champion. Who was that?

17 At the 1993 Royal Rumble, he got the better of a future Intercontinental champ. Who was that?

18 Things didn't go well for Hart at WrestleMania IX, though. He lost his title to the monstrous Yokozuna. But the unsmiling alien had some help from Mr. Fuji. How did he interfere?

19 Bret had another excuse for losing his title. What was that?

20 Hart's first reign as Federation Champion lasted 125, 150 or 175 days?

21 Bret was back on top again soon after. He was pronounced King of the Ring after beating which big man in the tournament finals?

22 Then it was on to Survivor Series '93, where he was joined by three of his brothers. Who were the other Harts?

23 Despite some difference between them, Bret and his brother Owen teamed up at the 1994 Royal Rumble, where they took on the Quebecers. When they lost, Owen blamed Bret. Why?

24 Bret had another engagement at that Royal Rumble - the battle royal. Whom did he eliminate just before he and Lex Luger hit the floor?

25 Bret regained his Federation Championship at WrestleMania X, thanks in part to Yokozuna's clumsiness. Can you explain?

◄ ANSWERS

LEX LUGER

NICKNAME:	Made in the USA
HOME TOWN:	Atlanta, Georgia
HEIGHT:	6'5"
WEIGHT:	265 pounds
MOTTO:	I'm 100% American made.

LEX LUGER

REBEL WITH A CAUSE

When it comes to hard-luck stories, Lex Luger seems to have written the World Wrestling Federation book on it. Having one of the most impressive physiques in the sport, Luger's torso of granite makes him one of the strongest superstars in the New Generation of the World Wrestling Federation. However, there is much more to Lex than just muscle. With the colors of red, white and blue pumping through his veins, Lex Luger has become a modern-day American hero. He has a deep belief in his country and the millions of people who call it home. He has made it very clear that he will fight for the American cause no matter how great the challenge is! Whether or not Lex's luck will turn around is anybody's guess, but as the Rebel with a Cause confidently states: "You've got to believe!"

ABOVE: Made in the USA Lex Luger is a sensational wrestler who has beaten some of the best athletes in the Federation.

Lex Luger has one of the most magnificently sculptured bodies in professional sports today.

Alundra Blayze is a woman of the '90s and an athlete women of all ages admire.

ALUNDRA BLAYZE

SMOKIN' FROM THE INSIDE OUT!

ALUNDRA BLAYZE

NICKNAME:	Woman of the '90s
HOME TOWN:	Tampa, Florida
HEIGHT:	5'9"
WEIGHT:	145 pounds
MOTTO:	Shoot for the stars.

Alundra's path to the pinnacle of her profession was anything but charmed. She was often the only woman training in sweaty wrestling gyms, where she learned to take a punch "like a man." After a short time on the American wrestling scene, she grew disappointed with the lack of emphasis on women in the sport. Driven by the desire to excel, Alundra traveled to Japan, where women's wrestling is regarded with the same respect as the men's.

Once again, however, Alundra found herself playing the role of the outsider. The established Japanese performers resented the stunning blonde from the States, and many frequently tried to cause her injury. Fortunately, Blayze endured, incorporating the Japanese martial-arts-based style into her technique.

Back in the United States, Alundra entered the World Wrestling Federation and exposed fans to a thrilling type of women's wrestling they'd never before seen. Although she lost the championship to Bull Nakano, she'll forever be regarded as the golden girl of the mat.

ABOVE: Alundra Blayze in action against Bull Nakano.

RAZOR RAMON

OOZING MACHISMO

The Bad Guy Razor Ramon has literally had to fight for everything he has ever gotten out of life. Today, that fight continues. Ramon, a two-time Intercontinental Champion, grew up in the barrios of Miami. He had to learn about life the hard way—on the street. Fighting for survival every day, Razor never backed down from anyone or anything. That attitude is still alive and well, living between the ropes of the World Wrestling Federation. At 6'7" and close to 300 pounds, Razor is an awesome force. The combination of brute strength and raw toughness has twice earned him gold in the Federation. Backed by a relentless style, the Bad Guy has proved time and time again that he can dish it out as well as take it. With the assistance of his patented finishing move fittingly called the "Razor's Edge," Ramon has defeated such adversaries as Heartbreak Kid Shawn Michaels, Big Daddy Cool Diesel, Bam Bam Bigelow and IRS.

RIGHT: The Bad Guy Razor Ramon is a two-time Intercontinental Champion.

RAZOR RAMON

NICKNAME:	The Bad Guy
HOME TOWN:	Miami, Florida
HEIGHT:	6'7"
WEIGHT:	287 pounds
MOTTO:	Say hello to the Bad Guy.

BULL NAKANO

HOME TOWN:	Tokyo, Japan
NICKNAME:	The Terror from the Orient
HEIGHT:	5'7"
WEIGHT:	220 pounds
MOTTO:	Alundra is mine!

The mighty Bull—weighing in at over 200 pounds—was always an intimidating presence in the ring. With her eyes smeared with gruesome face paint and her hair plastered high above her head, she viciously laces into her daintier foes, pounding them with the intensity of her namesake, the bucking bull.

From California to Connecticut, and Oregon to Oklahoma, Bull battled Alundra Blayze, with Alundra barely escaping with her title on numerous occasions. Finally, after months of petitioning World Wrestling Federation President Jack Tunney, Nakano was granted a title match in her home field—the Tokyo Dome. There, in front of 42,500 women's wrestling fanatics, the colossus from the Far East won the cherished crown.

With the belt since extended to fit around Nakano's waist, Bull vows to give no quarter to any of the pretenders to the throne. While women in other professions may be regarded as "the fairer sex," this mammoth monarch is determined to live up to her reputation as the Queen of Mean!

RIGHT: Bull Nakano won the World Wrestling Federation Women's Championship from Alundra Blayze in Japan in November 1994.

Bull Nakano is the current Federation Women's Champion. She is as mean as she is powerful.

BULL NAKANO

THE TERROR FROM THE ORIENT

The Heartbreak Kid Shawn Michaels is a brash and cocky superstar.

SHAWN MICHAELS

PROPRIETOR OF THE HEARTBREAK HOTEL

Although he comes to the ring with good looks, a sense of flair and arrogance more characteristic of rock stars than wrestlers, Michaels—known as the Heartbreak Kid—has the talent to back up the hype.

The 6-foot-1-inch, 234-pound former Intercontinental and Tag Team titleholder displays a ruggedness normally reserved for men not so preoccupied with their looks. He'll go toe to toe with more powerful foes, muscling them down to the canvas or pummeling them in out-of-the-ring brawls.

Michaels has even gained fame for his out-of-the-ring activities, hosting a segment on World Wrestling Federation programs called "The Heartbreak Hotel" and writing an advice-to-the-lovelorn column in World Wrestling Federation Magazine.

Nevertheless, those who've been betrayed by Shawn warn: "Never get too close to the Heartbreak Kid." After skyrocketing to greatness with Marty Jannetty—his tag partner in the Rockers—he turned on his teammate and humiliated him in public. Recently, he cultivated a feud with his longtime bodyguard, Diesel.

LEFT: Despite his arrogant personality, Shawn Michaels is nevertheless a gifted World Wrestling Federation superstar.

SHAWN MICHAELS

NICKNAME:	The Heartbreak Kid
HOME TOWN:	San Antonio, Texas
HEIGHT:	6'1"
WEIGHT:	234 pounds
MOTTO:	I'm the greatest thing there is on God's green earth!

OWEN HART

OWEN HART

NICKNAME:	King of Harts
HOME TOWN:	Calgary, Alberta, Canada
HEIGHT:	5'11"
WEIGHT:	227 pounds
MOTTO:	I'm the best Hart.

HAIL TO THE KING OF HARTS

After a spectacular start in his native Canada, Owen traveled to Germany, Mexico and Japan, learning the unique styles of those locations.

By the time the 5-foot-11-inch, 227-pound Owen entered the World Wrestling Federation, he possessed the experience of many wrestlers twice his age. However, it was Bret who continued to grab the headlines. Finally, jealousy and frustration drove Owen to take desperate measures. He viciously assaulted his older brother and dedicated himself to destroying Hit Man's career.

Owen's finest moment in the mat wars may have been when he defeated Bret in the opening match at WrestleMania X, although even then, he didn't get the satisfaction he craved. Later in that same evening, Hit Man captured the World Wrestling Federation Championship.

A few months later, Owen won the grueling King of the Ring tournament and confidently declared himself the "King of Harts." Unfortunately, despite his notable talents and track record, he continues to cringe when anyone reminds him that he's Bret's baby brother.

RIGHT: Owen Hart is known as the "King of Harts," after winning the King of the Ring Tournament in June 1994.

Although Owen "The King of Harts" Hart is a tremendous wrestler, he is a loathsome person, especially to his brother Bret.

Jim "The Anvil" Neidhart is as solid as he is mean. He weighs a whopping 280 pounds.

JIM "THE ANVIL" NEIDHART

THE INFAMOUS INSTIGATOR

Neidhart, who earned his nickname with a world record anvil toss, was once Bret "Hit Man" Hart's best friend and tag team partner. On several occasions, they won the Tag Team Title with their celebrated Hart Attack.

The Hart clan was initially delighted when Neidhart married one of Bret's sisters; however, when Hit Man's younger brother Owen decided to wage war on his older sibling, those sentiments changed.

For his own reasons, Neidhart took Owen's side. When the two brothers fought in a cage at SummerSlam '94, the 6-foot-1-inch, 281-pound Anvil jumped Bret after his victory, assisting Owen in pulling the Hit Man back into the pen for more torture.

Anvil not only earned the wrath of Bret but that of another brother-in-law, the British Bulldog. Yet Neidhart seems happier than at any other time in his career. Why the elation? "I guess I just like to stir things up," explains the goateed badman.

RIGHT: Jim "The Anvil" Neidhart is one sick puppy. This man has been known to pound his foes without mercy.

JIM NEIDHART

NICKNAME:	The Anvil
HOME TOWN:	Reno, Nevada
HEIGHT:	6'1"
WEIGHT:	281 pounds
MOTTO:	Yeah, baby!

Jeff Jarrett

AIN'T HE GREAT?

Jeff Jarrett—or Double J—claims to have been blessed with abilities in two fields. Not only is he a premier wrestler, but he insists that he's also a country music legend waiting to be discovered.

The rhinestone cowboy asserts that he's "using" the World Wrestling Federation to grab the attention of music promoters throughout the world.

Every month, he does a record review in World Wrestling Federation Magazine, in which he's quick to brand the most famous bands "frauds" and "has-beens." Double J confidently claims that no musician alive today is as gifted as he is.

Jarrett claims to have recorded an album entitled "Ain't I Great?" However, no one can find his CD *anywhere*!

Meanwhile, the 6-foot-1-inch, 230-pound native of Music City, USA, struts to the ring and usually rock 'n' rolls to victory. When he wins a match with his version of the figure-four leglock, he boasts that he's defeated another opponent with the "six string."

BELOW: Double J believes the powers-that-be in the country music business have "blackballed" him.

Double J Jeff Jarrett—that's J E double-F J A double-R E double-T—lives in Music City, USA.

JEFF JARRETT

NICKNAME:	Double J
HOME TOWN:	Music City, USA
HEIGHT:	6'1"
WEIGHT:	230 pounds
MOTTO:	Ain't I Great!

From the great state of Texas come the Smoking Gunns—Billy and Bart.

THE SMOKING GUNNS

BOTH BARRELS BLAZING IN QUEST FOR THE GOLD

Billy and Bart Gunn were both raised on the wide plains of Texas where, they say, everything was done better and bigger.

Because they are brothers who have been scuffling side by side since infancy, 254-pound Billy and 258-pound Bart are masters of teamwork. Between the ropes, they barely have to speak to each other; the two thrive on instinct.

In the midst of a match, one man will effortlessly lift an opponent off the ground, twirl him around and drape him across a knee, while the second Gunn drops down on the victim from the ropes. Other times, they'll use quick tags to bewilder their rivals, pinning them long before they even realize WHO or WHAT hit them!

The Gunns have been known to compare their tussles in the squared circle to the rodeos they entered as children. Regardless of the type of competition, Billy and Bart always return home with the blue ribbon.

RIGHT: The Smoking Gunns, Billy and Bart, are two of the toughest and most popular hombres in the World Wrestling Federation.

• • • • • • • • • • • • • • • • • •

"Yee-Haa!"

19

Doink the Clown, the Prince of Pranks, and his pint-sized powerhouse, Dink.

DOINK & DINK

THE JOKE'S ON THEIR OPPONENT!

The "clown prince of the World Wrestling Federation," Doink comes to the ring with one purpose: to instill laughter in the audience. Unfortunately for his foes, those chuckles are always gained at their expense.

Most fans think the team of Doink and Dink is all face paint and guffaws, but below the surface there's a *bona fide* wrestling talent. The 6-foot-tall, 243-pound Doink will astound an opponent by taking the man down to the mat with a classic maneuver like a fireman's carry or double leg pick-up. Almost always, the match ends with Doink delivering his "Whoopie Cushion," diving off the top rope and squashing the air out of a foe's stomach.

Periodically, little Dink has assisted Doink in tag team contests. While their opponents are quick to brand the tiny jester "a little pest," he's proved just as adept as his partner at garnering victories. In the World Wrestling Federation, "clown time" is fun time for this pugnacious pair—and misery for their foes.

RIGHT: Santa Claus gave Dink to Doink during 1993's Christmas season. Doink's "little buddy" has been by his side ever since.

DOINK	
NICKNAME:	The Prince of Pranks
HOME TOWN:	Unknown
HEIGHT:	6'2"
WEIGHT:	243 pounds
MOTTO:	Life's a joke.

1-2-3 KID

NEVER SAY DIE!

Tipping the scales at a mere 212 pounds, the 6-foot-tall 1-2-3 Kid was told by everyone that he had a slim chance of making it in the World Wrestling Federation. However, he ignored the warnings and compensated for his lack of size with a combination of guts, creative maneuvers and utter fearlessness.

The 1-2-3 Kid will take on anybody. Early in his career, he challenged rugged Razor Ramon, stunning the world—and earning the moniker 1-2-3 Kid—by putting the Bad Guy down for the three-count.

For a short while, the 1-2-3 Kid was co-holder of the World Wrestling Federation Tag Team Title with Marty Jannetty. Bret "Hit Man" Hart has called the dauntless competitor the "best pound for pound wrestler today.' Still, when the 1-2-3 Kid is ready for retirement, fans will remember him not for the titles or accolades but for his inspiring "never say die" attitude.

Excitement personified, the 1-2-3 Kid is the backbone of the New Generation.

LEFT: The 1-2-3 Kid may not be the biggest superstar, but he unquestionably has the most heart and guts.

• • • • • • • • • • • • • • • • • • • •

1-2-3 KID

NICKNAME:	Underdog
HOME TOWN:	Minneapolis, Minnesota
HEIGHT:	6'
WEIGHT:	212 pounds
MOTTO:	Never quit when you're down.

The Head Shrinkers, Fatu and Seone, hail from the island of Samoa in the South Pacific. They are managed by Captain Lou Albano.

THE HEAD SHRINKERS

SAMOANS ON THE HUNT!

HEAD SHRINKERS

Nickname:	The Samoan Savages
Home Town:	Samoa
Height:	Fatu - 6'2"
	Seone - 6'3"
Combined Weight:	587 pounds
Motto:	None

A generation ago, a tag team known as the Wild Samoans tore up the World Wrestling Federation. Today, their descendants, Fatu and Seone, have stepped into the gap left by the legendary Polynesians. In match after match, the pair mangles its adversaries like two predatory beasts skinning their dinner.

Fatu and Seone are well-schooled in the ways of the squared circle. Their trainer is Afa, one-half of the storied Wild Samoans, while Captain Lou Albano, the most successful manager in the history of the World Wrestling Federation, is at the team's helm.

At the conclusion of most matches, 6-foot-3-inch, 293-pound Seone batters an opponent with a combination of brawling and martial arts maneuvers while setting him up for the 6-foot-2-inch, 296-pound Fatu and his devastating splash off the top rope.

The Shrinkers' aggressiveness led them to the World Wrestling Federation Tag Team Title. Even after they lost the championship, the fans continue to cheer the duo's untamed tactics.

RIGHT: The Head Shrinkers, Seone and Fatu, are arguably the strongest tag team in the Federation today.

ADAM BOMB

THE CREATION OF DEVASTATION

ADAM BOMB

NICKNAME:	The Dean of Destruction
HOME TOWN:	Three Mile Island
HEIGHT:	6'7"
WEIGHT:	292.5 pounds
MOTTO:	I'm the creation of devastation.

ABOVE: Adam Bomb—who is the president of the Bomb Squad—makes his home on Three Mile Island.

Some wrestlers intimidate their rivals with remarkable skills, uncanny size and extraordinary power. Adam Bomb has all that and another weapon. The native of Three Mile Island is said to be radioactive.

Certainly, Bomb packs a mean blast between the ropes. At 6-foot-7 and 292 pounds, he towers over most of his adversaries and uses his size to the fullest advantage. When wrestlers run the ropes and attempt to shoulderblock this titan, they frequently end up on their backs—like those unfortunate enough to have been at ground level at Hiroshima and Nagasaki. When he finishes off a rival with his explosive Atom Smasher, observers can do little more than wait around and clear up the rubble.

Initially, Bomb's flammable personality caused many fans to jeer him whenever he stepped into the ring; however, since he separated from former manager Harvey Wippleman, he's accumulated a growing legion of devotees. The name of this burgeoning movement: the Bomb Squad.

The Creation of Devastation Adam Bomb is a lethal weapon in the World Wrestling Federation.

DUKE DROESE

"THE DUMPSTER"

CLEANING UP THE FEDERATION!

Duke "The Dumpster" Droese calls Mount Trashmore, Florida, his home.

DUKE DROESE	
NICKNAME:	The Dumpster
HOME TOWN:	Mt. Trashmore, Florida
HEIGHT:	6'6"
WEIGHT:	305 pounds
MOTTO:	One man's garbage is another's treasure.

"Time to take out the trash!" The slogan—heard in homes across the world every night after dinner—has become this unique competitor's rallying cry. Since he was a child—growing up, quite appropriately, in Mount Trashmore, Florida—the big Dumpster has been fascinated with garbage. After school, he'd run straight to the dump, astounding the sanitation workers with his unusual strength as he hurled about bales of trash.

When certain types of wrestlers began making a name for themselves in the World Wrestling Federation, Duke decided it was time to redirect his energies. Instead of focusing on inanimate piles of garbage, the 6-foot-6-inch, 305-pound Droese went after the human kind—wrestlers who habitually broke the rules, interfered in matches and punished opponents after the bell.

Psyching himself up by banging on a trash can on the way to the ring, Droese has had more than a whiff of success in the squared circle, depositing his foes in heaps after first laying them to waste.

RIGHT: Ever since he joined the Federation, Duke Droese has been "carting away" the trash, so to speak.

Tatanka, the Native American, turned his back on his people and his fans in 1994.

TATANKA

A HERO WHO FELL TO GREED

This 6-foot-tall, 250-pound member of the Lumbee tribe of American Indians came to the World Wrestling Federation exemplifying the very best of his culture. He drew on the ancient lessons of his ancestors to condition himself for the rigors of the squared circle and encouraged all young people to excel in education and always aim high.

Unfortunately Tatanka was corrupted by the almighty dollar. Prior to a SummerSlam match with the All-American Lex Luger, Tatanka was "purchased" by the Million Dollar Man Ted DiBiase. Luger went into the contest expecting a scientific match from Tatanka. Instead, he received a vicious attack at the hands of the sold-out turncoat.

Since then, Tatanka has offered no apologies while he continues to deposit DiBiase's riches in his Swiss bank account. As he continues to dominate opponents with his special finisher called the End of the Trail, he brags that his aim in life is now to accumulate as much wampum as possible.

RIGHT: Tatanka "sold out" to the Million Dollar Man's Corporation at SummerSlam '94.

TATANKA

HOME TOWN:	Pembroke, N. Carolina
HEIGHT:	6'
WEIGHT:	250 pounds
MOTTO:	I'm proud to be a RICH Native American!

TED DIBIASE

MONEY TALKS!

The Million Dollar Man Ted DiBiase is the CEO and president of the Million Dollar Corporation.

While all wrestling fans are well aware of DiBiase's prosperity, a smaller percentage realize the extent of his wrestling background. The Million Dollar Man is one of the few World Wrestling Federation superstars capable of boasting that both his father and his mother competed in the squared circle.

Even his harshest enemies concede that, without the bragging, DiBiase is one of the finest athletes ever to step through the ropes. He's come within a hair of taking the World Wrestling Federation Championship on many occasions and is a former co-holder of the Tag Team Title.

Recently, DiBiase has chosen to live a more leisurely life, opting to manage wrestlers rather than lock up with them. His stable includes man-monsters like Bam Bam Bigelow and King Kong Bundy, as well as the tough, versatile Tatanka.

The Million Dollar Man also has emerged as one of the most controversial color commentators in the television industry — lending a brand-new meaning to the term "money talks."

LEFT: The Million Dollar Man believes that "everyone has a price." He often goes to great lengths to prove it.

TED DIBIASE

NICKNAME:	Million Dollar Man
HOME TOWN:	Seasonal
HEIGHT:	6'3"
WEIGHT:	260 pounds
MOTTO:	Everybody's got a price!

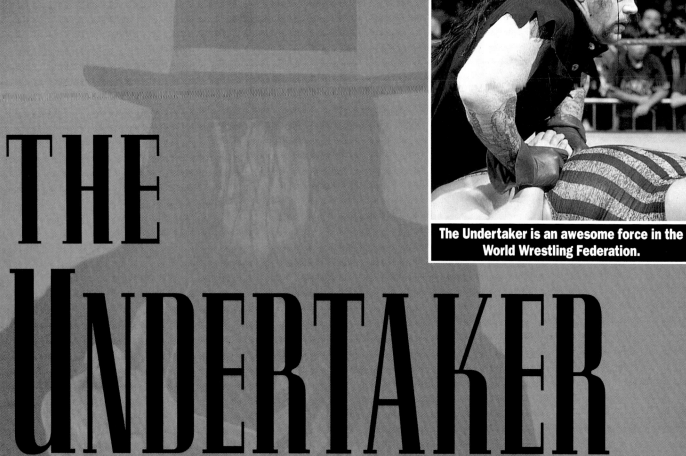

The Undertaker is an awesome force in the World Wrestling Federation.

THE UNDERTAKER

MYSTERIOUS MAN FROM THE DARK SIDE

Never in the history of the World Wrestling Federation has there ever been a character such as the Undertaker. Hailing from Death Valley, the Grim Reaper has always been surrounded with both mystery and mystique. Who is he? Where did he come from? Why is he here? Even today those answers remain unsolved mysteries. Accompanied by the keeper of his sacred urn, Paul Bearer, the Dark Man of so few words lets his actions do the talking. Though black clouds hover above him everywhere he goes, the Undertaker's career has been everything but gray. By using one of the most devastating finishing moves in wrestling today, the Tombstone, the Undertaker is THE MOST dominant force in the New Generation of the World Wrestling Federation!

RIGHT: From the Dark Side comes the incredible Undertaker—master of the Tombstone.

UNDERTAKER

NICKNAME:	Grim Reaper
HOME TOWN:	Death Valley
HEIGHT:	6'10.5"
WEIGHT:	328 pounds
MOTTO:	Rest In Peace...

"Rest In Peace"

BRITISH BULL-DOG

The British Bulldog is a former co-holder of the Tag Team Belts and a former Intercontinental Champion.

BEWARE THE ROYAL K-9

The British Bulldog a.k.a. Davey Boy Smith is more than just a former World Wrestling Federation Tag Team and Intercontinental Champion. He's an international celebrity, responsible for inserting a European catch-as-catch-can style into what had been largely considered an American game.

Smith and his partner Dynamite Kid first took the wrestling world by storm in the mid-1980s by combining strength with aerial moves to alter the way tag teams operated between the ropes.

However, fans clamored to see the Bulldog in individual competition, and when the 5-foot-11-inch, 253-pound Brit tried his hand as a singles competitor, he more than satisfied his devotees.

In an unforgettable contest, he went head-to-head against his brother-in-law Bret "Hit Man" Hart in front of a partisan crowd at London's Wembley Stadium. When it was over, Smith had captured the prestigious Intercontinental Title and forever engraved his name in wrestling's annals.

Recently, the English powerhouse has proved himself Bret's most valuable ally as the pair battles a contingent led by dissident family members Owen Hart and Jim "The Anvil" Neidhart.

RIGHT: The British Bulldog puts the pressure on brother-in-law Owen Hart in a grueling match.

BRITISH BULLDOG

HOME TOWN:	Manchester, England
HEIGHT:	5'11"
WEIGHT:	253 pounds
MOTTO:	The dog is on the loose.

❝ The dog is on the loose ❞

MEN ON A MISSION

TAKIN' IT TO THE STREETS

M.O.M.

NICKNAMES:	Mo: Harlem Hero
	Mabel: The Big Man
HOME TOWN:	Harlem, New York
HEIGHT:	Mo: 5'11"
	Mabel: 6'8"
WEIGHT:	Mo: 285 pounds
	Mabel: 503 pounds
MOTTO:	Whoomp, there it is!

Mo and Mabel—also known as Men on a Mission or M.O.M.—are from the mean streets of Harlem, New York. Their fast-talking manager, Oscar, grew up amid the poverty of south-central Los Angeles. They've all melded their experiences into a hard-driving style that combines rapping with wrestling.

Between the ropes, the 5-foot-11-inch, 285-pound Mo can floor an opponent with a figurative putdown—reducing the wrestler with a colorful comment or a literal one—while 6-foot-8-inch Mabel is capable of levitating his 503 pounds high above the canvas to blast a rival with a dropkick.

Everything about M.O.M. is unique, from the customized songs their manager Oscar composes before each match to the wrestlers' blond mohawks to their merging of the music and sports worlds. From the back streets of "the 'hood" to leafy suburban back yards, fans are rocking to the rhythm of Men on a Mission.

LEFT: Men on a Mission—Mo and Mabel—are one of the biggest tag teams of all time in the World Wrestling Federation.

Men on a Mission, Mo and Mabel are two rappin' homeboys from Harlem, New York.